New Hunger
Ella Duffy

smith|doorstop

Published 2020 by Smith|Doorstop Books
The Poetry Business
Campo House,
54 Campo Lane,
Sheffield S1 2EG
www.poetrybusiness.co.uk

ISBN 978-1-912196-31-9
Designed & Typeset by Utter
Printed by Biddles

Smith|Doorstop books are a member of Inpress:
www.inpressbooks.co.uk. Distributed by NBN International, 1 Deltic Avenue,
Rooksley, Milton Keynes, MK13 8LD.

The Poetry Business gratefully acknowledges the support of
Arts Council England.

Supported by
ARTS COUNCIL
ENGLAND

Contents

For Florence
and for my mother
with love

Odyssey

Sixteen, fearing the queerness you'd hooked,
cautiously, under your heart, you wonder
if this was how Odysseus felt, tied to a mast,
ears plugged with wax, as the ship he captained
tore across an ocean seized by siren, their salt song.
The ache for flesh that wasn't his own, forbidden.

You know how it feels to deafen yourself,
freeze thoughts of want before they warm
on your tongue. The fear that if you were
to unbind your hands, strike out for land,
you might drown ... or you'd reach them,
their chorus singing you in on a lifeline;
a kiss that tastes of the sea.

Faith

When you said *would you rather*
I believed in God or ghosts?

you were really asking if it were possible
to carry on if one of us believed
in something the other couldn't.

How lack of the same faith could be a religion
for new lovers, in those quiet hot weeks
spent in bars, between sheets.

So I paused, then prayed at your lips,
our breaths ghosting on my words.
Neither, I said, *both*.

Plum Picking

I hold your coffee as you reach
for the highest branch,
pluck a plum from its stem
and with your thumbs
pull the flesh apart.

You check for worms and wasps
then bite down, head tipped,
lips glossed with syrup
which I kiss, and with my teeth
steal the stone

from your mouth
to rest on my tongue
like a promise, a vow
passed between us, coloured
and perfumed with fruit.

Walks

While some things
offer mourning –

a widowed swan
or rain-downed bee –

bluebells

fuel their field
to sudden colour,

as if from under the soil
a match had sparked.

Tree

I waited so long for you
that I turned into a tree;

toes squirmed through soil,
ten roots to encounter the dead.

From my ankles up,
skin itched into bark;

a rash bubbled with moss.
Then cramp,

as each brown breath
rasped a limb;

armfuls of tight buds
ticking on their twigs.

So desire was sap
and language birds

pecking my scalp
under its wig of leaves.

And what was there to taste
other than mulch, worm,

the milky droppings
of an owl?

More to smell, hear;
the sweat and tread

of passersby who would
never be you.

Or when children strained
to climb my trunk,

dropped from branch to grass –
bright fruits –

I would wonder
if they were yours.

Blackbird

There are birds sewing together the margins
of leaves; eggs tucked in tree-top pockets.

I am eating pasta at the garden table
when your nest throws you up and over.

Barely enough plume to soften your back,
you are unlit coal.

If I make you a home of my palms
you will lose your wildness,

shrink like a bar of soap
passed between hands.

You play your lungs only once.
Above, feathers, a disgrace of notes.

Hunger has brought you into my lap.
Soon, I am offering tweezers of cat food.

I am no mother.
You are dead by morning.

Moss Children

are singing from the garden,
songs as low and quiet as damp.

Their tongues, foraged herbs,
are shaping ancient sounds. Soon,
the garden will be humming.

Moss children are standing
in the shade, feet threaded
to stone and bark, moving only
to bob for fistfuls of cress.

Watch the self-burial of rain.
Moss children soak it up
through their toes, blush
a deeper shade of green.
Sometimes, they cry for milk,

and mothers wake
believing their own babies
have wandered too far.
Stolen milk, spilt on the bank,
flowers to hemlock;
moss children laugh in the stream.

Mantis

She stills herself,
a green meditation,
angled with desire
for aphid, moth.

Icon, on guard,
she is threat posed
as prophet. A body
of tricks, mischief

made leaf, flowering
to thorn; a small
violence. Trauma
is feast.

Mantis, wild queen,
her face is geometry
at play; a compass
for the dead.

Tuna

Bluefin; barrel of salt; a barb
hooked to its gape; mouthful

of krill swilled between cheeks,
pooled on the tongue; last feed.

Last of its shoal, which once
blitzed through tides; a force

of tanks, in their element,
each armoured with a skirt

of yellow darts; fins drawn
to a point like arrowheads.

Silver keg, punctured, drained;
shy organs hauled from flesh,

swollen and scored, the rings
of a fingerprint. Then sea,

the colour of tin, then sky.
Then the whole world tin.

Butterfly Pinning

Relax the dead with damp towels,
ease their hinges;
wings will soften enough to spread.

Hang a board of mounted
butterflies opposite a mirror
as if they might admire themselves.

Call them perfect, but the room
is disturbed, throws the reflection
into corners.

In low light, these pinned shapes
could be folded paper. I am counting
the hours until nightfall.

Bite

In my dream, we shared a bed with a dozen bats,
each no bigger than a fig. And in my dream,
you told me to stay still, that the bats would hear
my rustling as moth wings;
                                  a flighted body
to snack on. But in my dream, I did move,
and, pinning itself to my chest, a leathery brooch,
was the smallest bat.
                            I woke unhurt, but still
you checked me over as I clawed at my breast
saying, *I have been bitten by a tiny waking.*

Chill

Medusa runs a bath
so hot it flays the scales
from her skin.

Soft, briefly more woman
than beast, she wanders
the house to suck

the stony fingers of her men.
One on the bed. One with his glass
raised to his lips. One in the hall,

gifted with grey flowers.
Her memories spit and hiss.
Loneliness is intimacy

told backwards. She tongues
their marble chests
like a graveyard dog.

Nightjar

The goats have gone blind.
Something awake after dark
has milked the pen dry.

Tonight, I stay up, walk
the sore field to find
a nightjar draining

a sheep; its routine
of pierce and suck,
suckle and sip, disturbed.

It stares, prehistoric, shakes
the cream from its beak
then allows the dark to steal

it back. Back home, you sleep
naked; breasts pale as milk
under my cheek, my hand.

XV

A tarot reader told me
I had the spirit of the devil,
that my partner should sleep
below a bag of boiled oats,
having nailed the heart
of a beetroot to bleed
down the door of our flat.

Fasting would starve it out,
she said. But in those empty
weeks I envied the dead,
till a pain in my gums
shucked the front teeth
from my mouth and a tongue
horse-whipped into the room.

My breath was a tannery.
How could I kiss her?
My lover came with ice
for the sweats; calm, somehow,
even as my lower back opened
to mud and a tail probed
its muscle towards the light.

The air was nettle.
Arms grew arms, grew
the medieval weight of a hoof.
From each pore, a thorn;
my body bristled,
a clove-studded ham.
I wouldn't be touched.

My eyes sunk in and back,
popped through the skull
like peeled fruits.
There would be no tears.
Sightless, my sense of smell
urgent as a horny stray,
I welcomed new hunger.

Preserved

She collects samples of herself –
discharge / dandruff / tooth.

She is charting a body through its cuttings,
and when there is infection, she stores it,
measures the movement of healing.

What does she learn about the body?
Its willingness to dismantle, its wetness
and stink. A deer sheds its antlers yearly

– bloody velvet pasted to bark / true bone
in a bush. She gathers her losses in glass.

Through a window, the spices and oils
of a home cook; but closer, consider
each bottle, each fermented pain.

Some will think it a clinic, others
knock on the door, opening
the mouths of their purses.

Salt

As a child she learnt
the taste of hurt;
brine stored under sight.

Then later, the comfort
of fish with olives,
its coastal tang.

She would seek its scent
on the skin of a lover,
tongue for it.

Or when it was spilt –
superstitious – throw it
over her shoulder.

She knew too many
who had lost everything
to rotten cities,

so they never looked back.
But when she turned,
saw her own city hot

and broken, she lost
herself; mistranslated
to salt.

The Old Drunkard

gawps, waits for the sky to uncork
a wine-cloud. In her lap, a flagon, cradled
like a stillbirth. She steadies it by the neck.

Her chiton slips from her shoulder, bares
a scaffold flagged by pleats, creased like the skin
which seeps down her cheeks in slack folds,
leaking towards the vessel's gut.

Eyes shrunk to garlic cloves and bleached
under lids, she slurs up at the moon.
If we stand here long enough,
she will start to sing.

Ouroboros

Think of this as hibernation;
learning to last on the body's
own larder of fat, like an adder,
overwintering; waking only
to shed the layers of skin
it no longer wants, or needs.
You begin to mistake hunger
for thirst, sate the ache
in your gut with citrus tea,
mugs of ice. The punnet
of grapes bruised by your bed;
a still life. Starving, you take
your feet, or tail, between
your teeth, then swallow.
Ouroboros, viper, faster,
feasting on muscle, bone,
you vanish into yourself;
a wraith now, wreath.

Injury

After the accident, they shaved your head
to its scalp – the caesarean purple of turnip –
and peeled the trauma from your skull.

That wild dark sleep. The heat of thought
dried on its wound and you woke wordless;
brain trussed like a fowl for a roast.

How much meat did they tear from your bone?
Which vein was threaded to sew up the skin?
They spooned the grease from your crown –

a cup of broth – skimming its stock to a bag
by your bed. We came with tulips;
split heads clotting the ward.

Saints

Lucy

A moth will blink its wings to trick.
You could have painted your palms
and the back of your neck
with new stares, and still they'd come.

They loved your eyes
and you loved to look.

Across the city, women locked
in marble were watched
watching, couldn't step
from their plinths. You itched
to thumb the sight from their lids.

And what was the moon that night
but an eye, sightless by morning?

You knew the world enough
to live with one less sense,
to sleep alone, the dish by your bed
serving its bloodstones, staring up.

Apollonia

Tilted by the chin,
probed with a blade,
a pomegranate will spit seed,
fleck a dress from white to red.

Would I have spent longer
preparing the fruit
had I known my last meal
would be the mouth's own harvest?

Say what you like,
before that, I was all smiles.

Noyale

Did she know then, with tendered neck,
that after the cut she would stand,
take up her head like laundry
and walk?

Not the first to hold her face to a crowd,
lick the sweat from her lips
and test her tongue for speech –
I must rest.

Her blood loosened the soil, whetting
the first spring. She knelt
at its bank, delivered
her wounded crown

like a newborn, washed rust from hair;
for a moment, allowed
herself to float as debris.
A falcon circled the field.

Euphemia

I'd like to believe it was true,
that after the wheel, the lions,
trained to maul, chose only
to lick the mesh of her back.

Scouring tongues softened,
tended the skin which hung
in threads. I'd like to believe
it helped, happened.

Halves

When the sea had me by the waist,
I cupped my hands between my legs
and pushed out my daughter.

She could not know then, as I licked
the caul from her scalp, that men
would rate her as rare leather,

boats sag their bellies of netting
for skin which might sieve
a woman;

the way her father had angled me
from my pod, turned me out of fur
to boast a girl.

I carried my child as a stone,
could never have seen us now,
mother and pup, the two halves

of a mussel shell, dipping
the shy grey of our backs
under foam and back into rumour.

Or

Under a kinder sun,
a lizard finds sleep
in the pleats of a flower.

We buy a house
with a garden.

Each morning,
I check the roses
for little dreamers,

pass this ritual on
to our children,

teach them to map
the last garden.
Our first-born stares

at a butterfly,
reading itself on a wall.

Shard

It was late when you called to say
you were on Southwark Bridge,

waving beneath a lamppost.
Third from the left.

So I stood at the window,
fifty floors up, pinned you

with the binoculars
which came with the room

then flashed the bathroom light;
morse code.

Around you, trains eased through
boroughs on wishbone tracks;

lanterns of Londoners
headed for home.

You danced on the road, blowing kisses,
giddy with seeing me,

your daughter, blinking my small light
down on the city;

the space between us swollen
and homesick, a mile long.

Acknowledgements

Thanks are due to the editors of *Ambit, The Aesthetica Creative Writing Annual, The Guardian Review, Live Canon 2019 Anthology, One Plum Poem, The Rialto* and *The Poetry Salzburg Review* in which some of these poems, or versions of them, first appeared.

With thanks to The Ginkgo Prize for Ecopoetry (2018) for awarding 'Tuna' runner-up; The Aesthetica Creative Writing Award (2018) for shortlisting 'Odyssey'; The Ambit Poetry Competition (2019) for awarding 'Halves' third place; The Live Canon International Poetry Competition (2019) for awarding 'Ouroboros' first place.

Personal thanks go to everyone at The Poetry Business; to my tutors at Goldsmiths for their advice and support; to friends and family who have encouraged me in the writing of these poems.